ARCHITECTS OF ASTRAL REALMS

Building Ethereal Spaces

D.R. T STEPHENS

S.D.N Publishing

CONTENTS

GENERAL DISCLAIMER

This book is intended to provide informative and educational material on the subject matter covered. The author(s), publisher, and any affiliated parties make no representations or warranties with respect to the accuracy, applicability, completeness, or suitability of the contents herein and specifically disclaim any implied warranties of merchantability or fitness for a particular purpose.

The information contained in this book is for general information purposes only and is not intended to serve as legal, medical, financial, or any other form of professional advice. Readers should consult with appropriate professionals before making any decisions based on the information provided. Neither the author(s) nor the publisher shall be held responsible or liable for any loss, damage, injury, claim, or otherwise, whether direct or indirect, consequential, or incidental, that may occur as a result of applying or misinterpreting the information in this book.

This book may contain references to third-party websites, products, or services. Such references do not constitute an endorsement or recommendation, and the author(s) and publisher are not responsible for any outcomes related to these third-party references.

In no event shall the author(s), publisher, or any affiliated parties be liable for any direct, indirect, punitive, special, incidental, or

1

other consequential damages arising directly or indirectly from any use of this material, which is provided "as is," and without warranties of any kind, express or implied.

By reading this book, you acknowledge and agree that you assume all risks and responsibilities concerning the applicability and consequences of the information provided. You also agree to indemnify, defend, and hold harmless the author(s), publisher, and any affiliated parties from any and all liabilities, claims, demands, actions, and causes of action whatsoever, whether or not foreseeable, that may arise from using or misusing the information contained in this book.

Although every effort has been made to ensure the accuracy of the information in this book as of the date of publication, the landscape of the subject matter covered is continuously evolving. Therefore, the author(s) and publisher expressly disclaim responsibility for any errors or omissions and reserve the right to update, alter, or revise the content without prior notice.

By continuing to read this book, you agree to be bound by the terms and conditions stated in this disclaimer. If you do not agree with these terms, it is your responsibility to discontinue use of this book immediately.

CHAPTER 1: INTRODUCTION TO ASTRAL ARCHITECTURE

Welcome to the wondrous world of astral architecture—a realm that fuses spirituality, metaphysics, and the art of creation. If you've ever meditated, practiced mindfulness, or explored various spiritual traditions, you may have already come across the concept of astral planes. But have you ever considered the potential of actively designing and constructing spaces within this otherworldly dimension? If that piques your interest, you're in for a transformative journey.

What is Astral Architecture?

In essence, astral architecture refers to the conscious creation of structures and spaces within the astral plane—a non-physical realm of existence that many believe is intimately connected to the soul and the universe. This is not architecture in the conventional sense. There are no physical bricks, no mortar, and no zoning laws to adhere to. Instead, it employs ethereal "materials," guided by intention, focus, and spiritual resonance.

The idea of creating spaces in non-material realms can be traced back to various mystical traditions around the world.

Shamanic practices, for instance, involve journeying to other realms where practitioners often encounter vivid landscapes and structures. Similarly, the Tibetan Buddhist concept of the 'Bardo,' an intermediate state between death and rebirth, is illustrated with complex palatial imagery in their sacred texts. Even the Kabbalistic Tree of Life in Jewish mysticism can be seen as an astral architecture blueprint that outlines various divine "spaces."

The Significance in Spiritual and Metaphysical Practices

The importance of astral architecture extends beyond mere curiosity or novelty. Many spiritual practitioners see it as an essential facet of their inner work for several reasons.

First, constructing astral sanctuaries can provide a safe space for meditation, introspection, and spiritual growth. Think of it as a sacred home away from home, where the usual distractions and disruptions of the physical world don't apply.

Second, building in the astral realm can help one manifest changes in the physical world. Many esoteric traditions suggest a strong interconnectedness between the astral and physical planes. A well-crafted astral space, therefore, could serve as a crucible for materializing intentions, insights, or energies into the earthly realm.

Third, the process of astral construction is itself a form of spiritual practice. It requires disciplined focus, clarity of intention, and a good understanding of metaphysical principles. It's not just about the final product—a beautiful astral temple—but also the self-transformative journey of creating it.

Verification Through Academic Research

While astral architecture is deeply rooted in various spiritual traditions, it's worth noting that the academic community has begun to explore related concepts, albeit cautiously. Research in fields like psychology, for example, has examined altered states of consciousness where individuals report experiencing vivid, otherworldly landscapes. While not directly corroborating the existence of the astral plane, these studies do highlight the pervasive human experience of 'other realms,' which could be tapping into similar phenomenological frameworks.

Similarly, scholars of religious studies have long examined the cosmologies of different spiritual traditions, noting the intricate descriptions of heavens, hells, and intermediary states. Again, while this does not scientifically validate the astral plane, it does emphasize its importance in the human spiritual narrative, spanning different cultures and epochs.

Charting the Course Ahead

So, whether you are a seasoned spiritual practitioner looking to deepen your metaphysical experiences or a curious newcomer enticed by the idea of creating your own astral domain, this book aims to be a comprehensive guide. We'll dive deep into techniques, unpack layers of sacred geometry, explore the use of elemental energies, and even consider the metaphysical equivalent of plumbing and electrical work in the astral realm. By the end, you should be well-equipped to construct your own ethereal spaces —be it a simple sanctuary for meditation or an elaborate astral cathedral.

And here we are, at the beginning of a mystical odyssey. May this chapter serve as the foyer to a grander astral edifice, one that we will build together, step by step, in the chapters to come. Welcome to "Architects of Astral Realms." Welcome to your journey of becoming an architect of the unseen, the unfathomable, and the profoundly sacred.

CHAPTER 2: THE ASTRAL PLANE: AN ARCHITECT'S CANVAS

Welcome back, dear reader! Now that you have a glimpse into the fascinating world of astral architecture, it's time to explore the terrain where you'll be laying your ethereal bricks and mortar: the astral plane. If you ever find yourself amazed at the sheer canvas that a physical world architect gets to work on, you'll be astounded by the limitless scope of the astral realm.

The Nature of the Astral Plane

Let's begin by understanding the astral plane's very essence. According to multiple schools of esoteric philosophy, the astral plane is a non-physical realm of existence sandwiched between the physical and the spiritual planes. Some regard it as the "emotional plane," given its close connection to human emotions, thoughts, and dreams. This dimension is malleable, shaped not only by collective human consciousness but also by individual intent and emotion.

Though science has not empirically validated the existence of the astral plane, it's a recurring concept in various religious and spiritual traditions like Hinduism, Buddhism, and Theosophy. Not just a figment of imagination, the astral plane is often described as more vivid than the physical world. It's a place where time and space are fluid concepts, bound more by perception than by any immutable laws.

Properties Unique to the Astral Plane

The properties of the astral realm differ profoundly from those of our familiar physical world. Think of it as a canvas with its own unique set of pastels and oils. First, there is the nature of matter—astral matter is subtle and highly responsive to thought and emotion. This makes it ideal for construction, as imagination becomes the hammer and nails. You're not bound by gravity or other natural laws; structures can float, walls can be translucent, and spaces can defy geometry.

Second, there's the fluidity of time and space. This unique quality allows you to create environments that change according to your whims or needs. You can craft rooms that expand or contract, or landscapes that shift from day to night in the blink of an eye. You could even design spaces where time appears to slow down or speed up.

Third, there is the malleability of form and function. A room can be both a tranquil sanctuary and a bustling marketplace, changing according to your intent or the collective intent of those present.

Why the Astral Plane is Ideal for Spiritual Architecture

The astral plane's fluidity and malleability make it a magnificent playground for spiritual architects. You're not just constructing spaces; you're creating environments for specific intentions—be it meditation, healing, or magical workings. Since the astral realm is highly sensitive to thoughts and emotions, the structures you build can become powerful conduits for spiritual energies.

The astral realm also provides a certain intimacy with one's higher self and the cosmic consciousness. When you build in the astral plane, you're laying down structures in a space that's intimately connected to your own spiritual journey. It's akin to having a dialogue with the Universe, expressed through your creativity.

The Astral Canvas and Its Limitations

While the astral plane offers boundless potential, it's important to note its limitations. The first is the issue of 'thought forms' and entities. The astral realm is home to a variety of beings— some benevolent, others not so much. Your constructions could attract or repel these entities, which is why setting intentions and protective measures are vital, topics we'll delve into in later chapters.

Another limitation is that the astral realm is subject to the collective unconscious to some degree. Thus, while individual will is powerful, it's not omnipotent. You may find that some structures are harder to maintain than others, especially if they go against collective beliefs or archetypes deeply ingrained in the human psyche.

Lastly, the astral plane, despite its flexibility, operates on a set of its own natural laws. Understanding these laws, which include karmic considerations and the rule of intent, is crucial for effective astral architecture.

Summary

The astral plane serves as a limitless canvas for your architectural endeavors, with its own unique properties and sets of challenges. With its malleable matter and fluid concepts of time and space, the astral realm is ideal for spiritual and metaphysical constructions. However, understanding its limitations and natural laws is key to becoming a proficient astral architect. Up next, we'll discuss how to actually get to this intriguing plane through the art of astral projection. But for now, sit back and ponder what wonders you would craft if the laws of physics were merely suggestions and your imagination was the only true limit.

CHAPTER 3: ASTRAL PROJECTION: THE GATEWAY TO ETHEREAL CONSTRUCTION

In the journey toward becoming architects of astral realms, understanding the mechanics of astral projection is critical. Astral projection is the gateway to ethereal construction. Without the ability to reach the astral plane, there is no canvas to paint on, no space to construct your dreams and meditative aspirations. This chapter explores the various methods and techniques of astral projection, highlighting the ways these approaches serve as the foundational entry point to creating stunning and deeply personal astral architecture.

The Fundamentals of Astral Projection

Astral projection is commonly understood as an out-of-body experience that allows you to travel or exist outside your physical body in a realm often referred to as the "astral plane." The concept exists across different cultures and has been discussed and documented in various spiritual traditions, from Hinduism and Shamanism to New Age philosophies. In essence, when you astrally project, you are moving your conscious awareness from your physical body to your astral body, often visualized as a tethered, luminescent form resembling your physical self.

Methods of Achieving Astral Projection

There are numerous approaches to achieve astral projection, each with its own set of prerequisites and challenges. Let's go over some of the most prevalent methods:

- The Rope Technique: This is perhaps one of the most beginner-friendly methods. It involves lying down in a relaxed state and imagining a rope hanging above you. In this meditative state, you picture your astral self-climbing the rope, which aids in separating the astral body from the physical one.

- The Vibrational State: This method focuses on entering a state where you become acutely aware of the natural vibrations of your physical body. By focusing on these sensations and enhancing them through meditation, you can facilitate the separation of your astral body.

- The Direct Method: Here, you lie down, enter a meditative state, and use focused willpower to move your astral body out of your physical one. This requires a high degree of mental discipline and is generally recommended for more experienced practitioners.

- Dream-Induced Astral Projection: Some people find it easier to achieve astral projection through lucid dreaming. In a lucid dream, you become aware that you're dreaming, and you can then attempt to convert this awareness into an astral projection.

It's advisable to experiment with different techniques to see which works best for you. Consistency and practice are key, as is finding a calm, uninterrupted space where you can practice regularly.

Significance of Astral Projection in Astral Architecture

The act of astral projection is the key to unlock the ethereal space where astral architecture takes place. It's a vehicle that takes you to the astral plane, where you can construct sanctuaries, temples, gardens, or whatever your heart desires. Think of it like commuting to a workspace; the astral plane is your construction site, and astral projection is your means of transportation.

Furthermore, proficiency in astral projection allows for greater control and finesse in your architectural designs. For example, if you master the art of moving fluidly in the astral realm, you can maneuver effortlessly through your constructions, making real-time adjustments and improvements. Your familiarity with the astral realm also lends you a 'local's perspective,' so to speak, which can be invaluable in crafting spaces that resonate with the natural frequencies of the astral plane.

Safety Considerations

While astral projection is generally considered safe, and there's no academic evidence suggesting physical harm from the practice, it's crucial to approach it with mindfulness. For beginners, it's beneficial to create a "protection circle" in the astral realm upon your first projections. This can be as simple as visualizing a circle of light around your astral form or as intricate as creating a circle imbued with symbols of personal or universal significance.

Also, always remember that your tether to your physical body is strong; you can return to it whenever you wish. However, like any form of travel, it's good to familiarize yourself with your 'destination' before setting off. Read widely on the subject, perhaps consult with seasoned practitioners, and approach the experience with an open but cautious mind.

Summary

Astral projection is not just an exploratory activity; it's a foundational skill for anyone serious about astral architecture. By mastering this ability, you are granted access to the astral plane, where you have the freedom to create, modify, and engage with your very own ethereal constructions. Techniques for astral projection vary in complexity and efficacy, so it's advisable to experiment and practice consistently. As you become more proficient in navigating the astral realms, your capabilities as an astral architect will only expand, allowing you to design and implement more intricate and resonant spaces for spiritual growth, healing, and beyond.

CHAPTER 4: FOUNDATIONS AND FRAMEWORKS: BASIC STRUCTURES IN ASTRAL ARCHITECTURE

Greetings, astral architects! By now, you have a firm grasp of what astral architecture is, the nuances of the astral plane, and the methods of astral projection that allow you to access this ethereal realm. With this understanding in place, let's delve into the "bricks and mortar" of astral construction: the foundations and frameworks that give shape and substance to your astral edifices.

Core Concepts of Astral Foundations

Much like physical architecture, the stability of your astral creation starts with a robust foundation. In the astral plane, your thoughts, emotions, and intentions serve as the core materials for this foundation. One could consider the astral plane a quantum canvas, sensitive to the slightest intention. Your clarity of purpose will serve as the bedrock on which you construct your astral haven. Without this, you may find your structures unstable, ephemeral, or, at worst, a misrepresentation of your original vision.

The Four Pillars of Astral Frameworks

When you're laying down the "structural beams" of your astral projects, think in terms of four essential pillars:

- Intentionality: This is the driving force behind any astral construct. What is the purpose of the sanctuary or temple you're building? Is it for meditation, ritual work, or perhaps for a peaceful retreat? Clearly defined intentions will guide the construction process and imbue your creation with purpose.

- Coherence: Your astral construction must have an internal logic to it, making it easier for you to navigate and utilize it for your specific needs. Lack of coherence could lead to confusion and could weaken the overall integrity of the structure.

- Resonance: This refers to the vibrational compatibility between you and the space you're creating. An effective astral construction should resonate with your energy signature or frequency, as well as the intended function of the space.

- Malleability: Unlike physical constructions, astral architecture is not static. It is a living, breathing entity that can adapt and change. While the core framework should be stable, allow room for adaptability to serve your evolving needs.

Anchoring Your Astral Space

Anchoring is the process of solidifying your astral structure in the plane. This often involves symbolic acts or rituals, similar to laying the cornerstone in a physical building. You can use symbols, sigils, or mantras that are meaningful to you to anchor your astral construction. The act of anchoring is akin to saving your progress in a digital file; it's a marker that ensures the stability and persistence of your ethereal architecture across multiple visits.

Plurality and Layering

Advanced practitioners often speak of the concept of layering within astral architecture. This involves creating multiple 'floors' or 'rooms' that serve different functions, or even connect to different spiritual realms. This is a complex endeavor and should be approached with caution. Having a coherent and well-anchored foundational layer is critical before adding additional layers to your astral edifice.

Materializing and Energizing Constructs

On the astral plane, the act of visualization is your primary construction tool. However, beyond simply visualizing, you can also channel specific energies into your construct to energize it. This is often achieved through focused meditation or through ritual acts carried out in the physical world that correspond to your astral construct. This added layer of energy enhances the potency and effectiveness of your astral space.

The Role of Archetypes and Symbols

Your foundation and framework can also benefit from universal archetypes and symbols, such as pyramids, circles, or the Tree of Life. These timeless shapes and forms have intrinsic power due to their collective unconscious resonance and can add an extra layer of stability and purpose to your astral construction.

Potential Hazards

While the astral plane is a realm of limitless creativity, it is also sensitive to your subconscious fears and insecurities. These can inadvertently find their way into your astral constructions, creating unintended traps or vulnerabilities. Be mindful of your emotional and mental state during the construction process. Regular cleansing and grounding techniques can help mitigate these risks.

In summary, understanding and implementing strong foundations and frameworks are critical to the longevity, utility, and spiritual potency of your astral constructions. By focusing on intentionality, coherence, resonance, and malleability, you lay down a robust framework that not only meets your immediate needs but also adapts to your evolving spiritual journey. Now that you have these building blocks in place, you're prepared to explore the more nuanced aspects of astral architecture, such as sacred geometry, elemental incorporation, and interior design, which we'll discuss in the subsequent chapters. So gear up, astral architects, as we move into the intricacies that transform mere structures into sanctuaries of spiritual enrichment!

CHAPTER 5: SACRED GEOMETRY IN ASTRAL DESIGN

Welcome to the mesmerizing realm of sacred geometry, where form meets meaning, and where design transcends simple aesthetic gratification to embody spiritual significance. Sacred geometry has been an elemental part of various spiritual traditions, from the mystical Kabbalah to ancient Hindu and Buddhist philosophies, as well as the Hermetic principles in the Western esoteric tradition. In this chapter, we will dive deep into how this ancient wisdom can be applied to astral architecture, enriching not just the structural aspect of your astral creations, but also enhancing their energetic resonance.

The Meaning Behind Shapes

The basic geometric shapes hold certain universal meanings that transcend cultural boundaries. Circles often symbolize eternity, unity, and completeness, given their unending form. Squares can denote stability and grounding because of their equal sides and angles, echoing the Earth's cardinal directions. Triangles often symbolize change and progression; their form implies movement and ascension, especially when pointed upwards. Understanding these foundational meanings can help you decide on the form your astral structure will take.

The Golden Ratio and Fibonacci Sequence

The Golden Ratio, an irrational mathematical constant approximately equal to 1.618033988749895, emerges often in nature, art, and architecture. Plants, seashells, and galaxies exhibit this ratio. It's believed that designs based on this ratio have a harmonious and aesthetically pleasing effect. In the realm of astral architecture, using the Golden Ratio could resonate with natural laws and universal beauty, aiding the flow and balance of energies within your astral space.

Similarly, the Fibonacci Sequence is a series of numbers in which each number is the sum of the two preceding ones, usually starting with 0 and 1 (0, 1, 1, 2, 3, 5, 8, ...). The Fibonacci Sequence is naturally aligned with the Golden Ratio; as you go higher in the sequence, the ratio between consecutive Fibonacci numbers approximates the Golden Ratio. It's another tool in your design arsenal that can add mathematical beauty and mystical significance to your astral structures.

Platonic Solids: The Building Blocks of the Universe

In the realm of sacred geometry, the five Platonic solids hold a special place. They are the tetrahedron (4 faces), hexahedron or cube (6 faces), octahedron (8 faces), dodecahedron (12 faces), and icosahedron (20 faces). Each of these geometric forms is a polyhedron, which means that its faces are congruent regular polygons, and the same number of faces meet at each vertex. These solids are seen as the building blocks of the universe in various philosophical systems.

When applied to astral architecture, each Platonic solid could serve a specific purpose or evoke a particular type of energy. For example, the cube could be used to create a sense of stability and grounding, whereas the icosahedron might inspire elevated states of consciousness or spiritual growth.

Incorporating Mandalas and Other Complex Forms

Mandalas are intricate designs often used as spiritual symbols and tools for meditation. They usually consist of a square with four gates containing a circle with a center point. In astral architecture, mandalas can be employed in the design of floors, ceilings, or even the overall layout of a structure. They can create a harmonious energy and serve as a focal point for meditation and other spiritual activities within the astral space.

Color and Vibration in Sacred Geometry

Color has its place in the design process as well. Each color has its frequency and vibrational quality, adding another layer to the complexity and effectiveness of your astral structures. For instance, violet is often associated with spiritual awakening, while green might relate to healing and balance.

Summary

The nuances of sacred geometry offer profound ways to enhance your astral architecture. Whether it's the foundational significance of basic shapes, the harmony of the Golden Ratio and Fibonacci Sequence, the elemental energies of Platonic solids, or the spiritual focus of mandalas, each geometric aspect carries its vibration and meaning. When used judiciously, these principles not only amplify the structural integrity of your astral constructs but also enrich their spiritual potency. Take your time to explore these ideas; after all, the astral realm isn't bound by the limitations of physical space and time. Your only limits are your imagination and willingness to experiment.

CHAPTER 6:
BLUEPRINTING
THE ASTRAL

Welcome to Chapter 6 of "Architects of Astral Realms: Building Ethereal Spaces." In this chapter, we'll delve into one of the most fundamental yet often overlooked steps in creating astral architecture—blueprinting the astral space. Just as architects in the physical realm use detailed blueprints to guide construction, a well-crafted blueprint will be invaluable as you undertake your ethereal building project. We'll explore why this planning phase is so important, how to go about it, and techniques to make it effective.

The Importance of Blueprinting

As you embark on your journey to construct astral spaces, it's tempting to dive right into the act of building. Yet, like any complex task, planning is crucial. Blueprinting, in this context, serves multiple purposes:

- Clarity of Vision: A detailed blueprint helps you crystallize your vision, making it easier to bring into existence.
- Alignment with Intent: The planning process allows you to align the astral construct with your spiritual or metaphysical goals.

- Efficiency: Knowing what you intend to build reduces the chances of errors or the need for revisions later on.
- Energetic Consistency: A planned space ensures that the energies within it are cohesive and harmonized, fulfilling the intended purpose with greater efficacy.

The Process: Mental Maps to Ethereal Constructs

- Conceptualization: This is the initial brainstorming phase where you imagine the kind of astral space you wish to create. Sketching or jotting down ideas can help manifest them more tangibly.

- Consultation with Spirit Guides or Higher Self: If you work with spiritual guides or consult your higher self during astral journeys, this would be a good time to seek guidance. They may offer valuable insights into the functionality or sacred geometry that would most benefit your intended space.

- Energetic Analysis: Determine the types of energy that will reside or flow within this space. It could be a place for calm reflection, intense spiritual work, or anything in between.

- Detailed Design: After gathering all the information, refine your vision. This is the time to decide on the elements of sacred geometry, energies, and any functional components like gates, portals, or altars.

- Alignment Check: Before finalizing your blueprint, ensure that every element aligns well with the overarching theme or purpose of the space.

Visualization Techniques for Effective Blueprinting

Visualizing your astral construct in vivid detail can be a challenging but rewarding exercise. Various techniques can aid in this process:

- Meditative Journeying: In a meditative state, journey to the astral realm and visualize laying down the blueprint in that space.

- Mind Maps: Create a mind map that outlines the different areas or components of your astral space and how they interconnect.

- Astral Trial Runs: Once you have a preliminary blueprint, make a few astral trips to test the structure. Note how it feels energetically and make adjustments as needed.

- Ritual Invocation: Some practitioners find it useful to perform a ritual that formally establishes the blueprint on the astral plane. This could involve lighting specific incense, chanting, or using specific crystals as a focus point.

Cross-Referencing with Sacred Geometry and Energetic Needs

By now, you've probably chosen certain sacred geometric forms to include in your astral construction, as covered in Chapter 5. During the blueprinting stage, cross-reference these choices with the intended energetic needs of your space. For instance, if your sanctuary is meant for healing, geometric forms that are commonly associated with healing energies, such as the circle or the vesica piscis, can be explicitly included in the blueprint.

Pitfalls to Avoid

- Overcomplicating the Design: While it's exciting to create an intricate astral space, complexity should not come at the cost of functionality or energetic harmony.

- Inconsistency: Consistency in design and intent enhances the energy of the space. Avoid frequent changes in the blueprint once construction starts, as it could disrupt the energy flow.

Summary

Blueprinting is an integral part of astral architecture. It ensures that the vision for your ethereal space is clearly mapped out and aligns well with your spiritual or metaphysical goals. The process involves conceptualization, consultation, energetic analysis, detailed design, and a final alignment check. Techniques like meditative journeying, mind maps, astral trial runs, and ritual invocation can aid in effective blueprinting. Paying attention to potential pitfalls like overcomplication and inconsistency will save you time and energy, making your astral construction project more fulfilling and effective.

CHAPTER 7:
ASTRAL MASONRY:
CRAFTING WALLS
AND BOUNDARIES

Welcome to Chapter 7! If you've been following along, you're now familiar with the fundamentals of astral architecture, the planning phase, and even the intricacies of sacred geometry. With a blueprint in hand and a foundational understanding of the astral realm's nuances, you're ready to dive into the constructive aspect of your ethereal endeavors. This chapter will focus on the techniques for creating walls and defining spaces in the astral plane. Think of this as the "masonry" phase of your astral construction.

The Importance of Boundaries in Astral Spaces

In astral architecture, walls and boundaries serve as both functional and symbolic elements. Functionally, they delineate the astral space you're creating, offering a clear demarcation between your sanctuary and the surrounding astral environment. Symbolically, these walls often resonate with protective energies, acting as shields against external influences that could be disruptive or harmful.

Some practitioners argue that the notion of walls or boundaries could seem antithetical to the boundless nature of the astral plane. However, the counterargument is that even in a space of infinite possibility, defining a "here" and "there" adds significance and purpose to your creation. It offers a controlled environment where intentions can more effectively manifest.

Choice of Materials: More Than Meets the Astral Eye

The first step in astral masonry is selecting the material you envision for your walls. You're not limited to bricks and mortar here; you could opt for walls made of light, flowing water, or even intangible elements like sound or emotion. The material you choose should align with the overall intention and purpose of your astral space.

- Light: Walls made of light can signify purity, divine connection, or enlightenment.
- Natural Elements: Earth, water, or even foliage can represent groundedness and a connection to Mother Earth.
- Sound: Walls of chants, hymns, or natural sounds like the rustling of leaves or the flow of water can create a harmonious atmosphere.

The Process of Construction: Visualization Techniques

Constructing walls in the astral plane largely relies on the power of visualization. Unlike physical construction, there are no tangible materials or tools involved. Here, your mental acuity is your greatest asset. The clarity with which you visualize the walls coming into existence, layer by layer or element by element, directly impacts their stability and effectiveness.

- Firm Intent: Start with a clear, unwavering intention that the wall should exist.

- Detailed Visualization: Bring the material you've chosen into your mind's eye. See its texture, its color, and its form. Imagine yourself or your astral self laying the materials down, one layer at a time.
- Energetic Infusion: As the wall takes form, imagine infusing it with energy that aligns with your intention. Visualize this energy as a color or as light permeating the structure.
- Seal the Deal: Once the wall is complete, imagine sealing it to lock in the energy and stabilize its form. Some practitioners use imagined sigils, words of power, or simply a burst of intense emotional or spiritual energy for this purpose.

Synergizing Boundaries with Sacred Geometry

If you've absorbed the concepts from Chapter 5, you might want to integrate sacred geometry into your astral masonry. For instance, if your astral sanctuary is based on the Flower of Life, the walls could be visualized as extensions of its lines and curves, maintaining the pattern's symmetry and harmony.

Astral Walls are Fluid Constructs

Remember, one of the beautiful things about astral architecture is its malleability. Your walls can be as permanent or as temporary as you wish them to be. They can be porous to let in specific energies while blocking others, or they can be solid, unyielding fortresses, depending on your needs and intentions.

Summary

Crafting walls and defining spaces within the astral realm can be a profoundly rewarding experience, imbued with both functional and symbolic significance. The choice of materials, the method of construction, and the energy you infuse into your astral walls all contribute to the potency and purpose of your sacred space. By masterfully combining these elements, you not only define your sanctuary but also provide it with a distinctive identity that aligns with your spiritual aspirations. Happy building!

CHAPTER 8: ELEMENTAL ALCHEMY: INCORPORATING EARTH, AIR, FIRE, AND WATER

Welcome back, intrepid architect of astral realms! By now, you've traversed the basics of astral architecture, learned about the significance of sacred geometry, and even dabbled in crafting walls and boundaries in the astral plane. As we move forward on this exciting journey, it's time to introduce a more nuanced layer to your ethereal constructs—Elemental Alchemy. In this chapter, we'll discuss the importance of incorporating the classical elements—Earth, Air, Fire, and Water—into your astral structures for added potency and purpose.

The Importance of Elemental Energy in Astral Architecture

Elemental energies serve as the building blocks of both the physical and spiritual worlds. In many esoteric traditions, these elements represent different states of being and the natural forces that govern our existence. By consciously incorporating elemental energies into your astral constructs, you can create a space that resonates on a multi-dimensional level. Whether you're working on a sanctuary, a temple, or any other astral structure, aligning it with elemental energies will bring a depth and resonance that simply visual or geometrical approaches can't match.

Earth: Stability and Grounding

The element of Earth is synonymous with stability, grounding, and nurturing energies. When incorporated into your astral constructs, Earth energy can provide a sense of rootedness and tranquility. In practice, you might visualize materials like stone or soil while meditating on Earth's characteristics. For instance, if you're building a meditation chamber within your astral sanctuary, consider using "astral stones" or "earthly soil" as the floor, or perhaps add "rocky formations" around the boundaries. This helps create a space where you can focus, meditate, and connect with your inner self while being "grounded" in the astral plane.

Air: Fluidity and Mental Clarity

In contrast to Earth's solidity, Air embodies movement, change, and mental clarity. It is the element that governs thoughts and communications. To introduce Air into your astral architecture, you might envision open spaces, perhaps with "astral wind" gently flowing through your structures. You could also "construct" windows or vents that allow for the free circulation of air. A room infused with the energy of Air would be ideal for intellectual pursuits, brainstorming, or engaging in conversations with other astral entities.

Fire: Transformation and Willpower

Fire, the element of transformation and willpower, is an excellent catalyst for change. It represents our drive, passion, and determination. When building areas intended for rituals, initiations, or any transformative processes, the energy of Fire can be remarkably effective. Visualize bright, flaming torches or even a central hearth where the "astral fire" burns eternally. The very act of including Fire within your astral construct can amplify the power of your intentions and rituals, imbuing them with transformative potential.

Water: Emotional Depth and Healing

Water symbolizes the emotional aspects of our being and the mysteries of the subconscious mind. It is closely related to the concepts of healing, intuition, and emotional balance. To include the energy of Water, visualize streams, ponds, or even small waterfalls within your astral construct. A room that incorporates Water would be excellent for healing rituals, emotional balance, and deep introspection.

Crafting Elemental Balance

The true beauty of incorporating elemental energies comes from crafting a harmonious balance between them. For instance, a room intended for meditation could blend Earth for grounding, Air for mental clarity, and Water for emotional balance. The key is to consider the purpose and function of each space within your astral construct and to align it with the appropriate elemental energies.

While the act of elemental incorporation is deeply personal and intuitive, the intentionality behind it is what brings life to your astral creations. You can blend these elemental energies in infinite ways, limited only by your imagination and the depth of your understanding of these primordial forces.

Summary

Incorporating elemental energies into your astral architecture isn't just a flourish or a gimmick—it's a means of bringing your ethereal spaces into alignment with the natural universe, enhancing their potency, and making them resonate on multiple dimensions. By understanding and working with the elements of Earth, Air, Fire, and Water, you enrich the narrative of your astral constructs and engage in an age-old practice that spans across various spiritual traditions and esoteric philosophies. So, as you go back to your astral drafting table, consider the elements as your new set of tools, each one holding its unique set of qualities to augment the power and purpose of your astral creations.

CHAPTER 9: INTERIOR ASTRAL DESIGN: CRAFTING SACRED SPACES WITHIN

Welcome to a chapter that unfolds the nuanced art of interior astral design. While previous chapters have provided you with the foundational knowledge and techniques for creating astral structures, now it's time to breathe life into these spaces. Yes, think of it as adding furniture to a newly built house. We're going to explore the inner sanctums, altars, and various layouts that can enhance the overall experience of your astral edifice. Let's delve into the creation of these sacred interior spaces within your astral temple or sanctuary.

Understanding the Purpose of Interior Design in Astral Architecture

The idea behind crafting the interior of your astral temple is to create a designated space for specific activities, intentions, or rituals. For example, a well-designed altar can amplify the effectiveness of your magical workings, while a meditation sanctum enhances introspective activities. Like in physical spaces where the arrangement and aesthetic of furniture can influence our mood and efficiency, the interior design of your astral architecture does the same, albeit in an ethereal form.

The Astral Altar: Your Centerpiece

The altar is often considered the focal point within an astral temple, serving both functional and symbolic roles. You can design your astral altar according to the purpose it serves—be it for magical rituals, offerings, or contemplative activities. The elements you include can be deeply personal, including representations of gods or goddesses, magical tools like wands or athames, and symbolic artifacts like crystals or pentagrams. The configuration and design can be as minimalistic or intricate as you wish, depending on your practice and preference.

Crafting Inner Sanctums: Specialized Areas for Specific Purposes

Within the astral temple, you may also desire sanctums or specialized areas dedicated to particular activities. For instance, a healing chamber filled with ethereal herbs and incense can serve as a sanctuary for rejuvenation, while a library filled with astral manuscripts could facilitate wisdom and knowledge-seeking. These sanctums help segregate activities within your astral edifice, making the temple versatile and multi-purpose.

Designing with Astral Aesthetics

When we think about aesthetics in the physical world, concepts like color theory, texture, and form come to mind. In the astral plane, these principles might manifest differently, given the ethereal nature of the realm. You can use various shapes and arrangements that hold symbolic or energetic significance in your spiritual tradition. Color, too, is powerful; soft pastel shades could foster a sense of peace, while vibrant reds could invoke passion or power. The aesthetics in astral spaces are malleable and adaptable to your unique spiritual needs.

Astral Décor and Symbolism

In your astral interior, décor serves a function beyond mere aesthetics—it can also incorporate additional symbolic or magical significance. For instance, using a recurring symbol like a lotus flower across the temple might serve as a continual reminder of purity and spiritual unfoldment. Small astral artifacts, perhaps a chalice or a sword, placed tactically can reinforce specific energies or facilitate ritualistic work. These elements add layers of meaning and resonance to your astral space, making it not just beautiful but also richly significant.

Summing it Up

In this chapter, we've discussed how to design and enrich the interiors of your astral structures. While the exterior may set the boundary and overall vibe, the interior is where most of your activities and rituals will take place. From the choice of décor to the function of various chambers, everything contributes to the effectiveness and sanctity of your astral temple. Crafting an interior that resonates with you is not just a matter of aesthetics, but of creating a harmonious energetic environment conducive to your spiritual practices. As you decorate your astral interiors, you'll find that these spaces become vibrant extensions of your inner self—places of immense value and meaning in your spiritual journey.

CHAPTER 10: ASTRAL GARDENS AND NATURAL ELEMENTS

Introduction

After diving deep into the realms of elemental alchemy and interior astral design, you might find yourself wondering, "What about the natural world?" The answer lies in the incorporation of gardens and natural elements into your astral architecture. Nature has always played a vital role in spiritual practices, grounding us in the present moment and inviting us to connect with the cycles of life. It's only logical, then, to consider how these elements can be woven into the fabric of your ethereal spaces. This chapter aims to provide insights into the importance, the methods, and the nuanced considerations of including nature in your astral constructs.

The Importance of Natural Elements

Whether it's the symbolism of a tree's roots reaching deep into the Earth or the tranquil qualities of flowing water, natural elements have been revered in various spiritual traditions for centuries. In the astral realm, the incorporation of these elements serves multiple purposes:

- Balance and Harmony: Integrating natural elements

helps in maintaining the energetic balance of your astral space. The five elements—Earth, Water, Fire, Air, and Ether—can act as grounding forces.

- Aesthetic Beauty: The artistic aspect of gardens and landscapes add to the overall allure and charisma of your astral domains, making them even more appealing to the astral visitor.

- Spiritual Significance: Many cultures believe that certain plants, trees, and natural formations hold spiritual power. Incorporating these into your astral garden can serve as a potent focus for your spiritual practices.

Choosing Your Flora and Fauna

The astral plane offers endless possibilities; you're not confined to the earthly definitions of plants or animals. Here are some steps to help guide you:

- Spiritual Resonance: Before choosing, contemplate the spiritual resonance you wish to establish. Plants like the lotus in Eastern spirituality or the oak in Celtic traditions carry particular symbolism.

- Functionality: Some plants are known for their healing properties, some for their protective qualities. Do your research to find what suits your purpose.

- Personal Connection: Your own affinity towards certain elements of nature should not be overlooked. Personal connections deepen the experience and facilitate a stronger bond with the astral construct.

Elemental Compatibility

Incorporating elements like Fire or Water comes with the task of ensuring compatibility with the existing elements in your astral space. For instance, you wouldn't place a fire pit next to a water pond unless you're specifically working on balancing opposing elements. The cohesion of elements adds to the fluidity and overall harmony of the realm you're creating.

Astral Landscaping: Techniques and Tools

This isn't traditional gardening; it's a play of energy, intention, and imagination. Visualization remains your main tool, aided perhaps by meditation or ritual to deepen the experience.

- Mapping: Just like your initial blueprint, a detailed map helps you place your trees, ponds, or mountains.

- Elemental Infusion: As you create, imagine infusing elements into your constructs. Envision the life-giving energy of Earth in the soil or the cleansing powers of Water in a waterfall.

- Energy Anchoring: Once the visualization is complete, mentally or energetically anchor the constructs into your astral space, setting the intention for their longevity and influence.

Maintenance and Energetic Upkeep

While astral constructs don't need watering or pruning, they do require energetic upkeep. Regular visits, along with reinforcing intentions and re-infusing energy, ensure the astral garden retains its vibrancy. If you've set protective barriers in earlier steps, extend these to cover your new natural elements.

Summary

Adding natural elements to your astral architecture is more than just an aesthetic choice; it's an intricate endeavor that requires thoughtful planning and a deep understanding of the significance of nature in spirituality. By selecting elements that resonate with your spiritual objectives, ensuring elemental compatibility, and employing potent visualization techniques, you create an astral garden that not only enhances the beauty of your ethereal realm but also serves as a powerful tool for spiritual development. As you step into the realms of astral landscaping, you're not just playing the architect; you're embracing the role of an astral gardener, cultivating a sanctuary that nurtures both the soul and the senses.

CHAPTER 11: GATES, PORTALS, AND TRANSITIONS

Introduction

Imagine the joy and awe you experience when you stand before an imposing castle gate or a delicately crafted archway in a physical environment. These entrances serve as the threshold between the outer world and the inner sanctum. In the realm of astral architecture, gates, portals, and transitions serve similar purposes. They not only contribute to the aesthetic appeal of your astral spaces but also provide functional roles in connecting different realms or dimensions within the astral plane. In this chapter, we delve into the nuances of creating these entrances and exits, adding layers of functionality and aesthetic depth to your astral structures.

The Aesthetic Dimension: Designing Gates and Portals

In physical architecture, the design of gates and portals often reflects the ethos of what lies behind them. The same can be said for astral architecture. Whether you prefer an archway filled with spiraling fractals or a simple, elegant passage adorned with symbols of personal significance, the visual characteristics of these entryways serve to set the tone for the journey ahead.

Materials can vary widely, depending on your intention and

aesthetic preference. You could envision walls made from crystalline substances emitting soft light or perhaps gates composed of flowing water that parts as one approaches. The visual elements often carry symbological meanings, derived from either universal archetypes or personal symbolism. For instance, a gate shaped like a lotus might symbolize purity and spiritual unfolding, aligning the visitor's thoughts with these qualities as they pass through.

Functional Aspects: Purpose-Driven Transitions

Gates and portals are not just for show; they also serve critical functional roles in your astral architecture. These could range from regulating the flow of energies into and out of your astral space to serving as waypoints for quick travel between disparate areas within or even outside your construction. Essentially, these entryways can act as filters or conduits, depending on how you design them.

Just like a well-placed door can change the flow of traffic in a physical building, a strategically located portal can influence the energy currents in your astral temple or sanctuary. The placement can be determined by various factors like the intended flow of chi, prana, or other life-force energies within your astral space. If designed appropriately, a portal could channel positive energies into a specific chamber for healing or meditation, enhancing the effectiveness of your astral constructs.

Linking Multiple Locations: The Interconnected Web

One of the fascinating aspects of astral architecture is the ability to connect different locations in a nonlinear manner. In the physical world, rooms must be adjacent or stacked to allow movement between them. However, in the astral realm, a gate could potentially link two entirely different spaces or even dimensions, irrespective of their 'geographical' locations in the

41

astral world.

To achieve this, one might employ sigils, runes, or incantations that act as 'coordinates' for these translocational gates. This requires a deep understanding of the metaphysical laws governing astral travel, as well as considerable focus and intention during the construction process. The design of these portals often incorporates specific symbols or geometric shapes that resonate with the target location, providing a form of 'astral GPS' that guides the traveler's journey.

Subtleties of Transition: Crafting Mood and Experience

Creating a portal or gateway is not just about designing the physical (or in this case, astral) structure. It also entails curating the experience of transition. As one passes through a gate, they might feel a shift in temperature, notice a change in lighting, or experience a subtle lift in their emotional state. These are all elements that can be designed intentionally.

To craft such nuanced transitions, you could integrate various sensory stimuli in and around the portal. Fragrances like incense could waft through the gateway, or ethereal music could accompany the traveler's movement. Even the texture of the floor could change, symbolizing the shift from one state or space to another. All these contribute to a more profound and transformative journey within your astral spaces.

Summary

Gates, portals, and transitions serve as the gatekeepers and connectors in your astral architecture, inviting both aesthetic beauty and functional utility into your ethereal spaces. From setting the visual and emotional tone to managing energy flow and linking disparate astral realms, these elements are integral to the completeness and effectiveness of your astral constructs.

As you ponder the design of your next astral project, consider the profound impact that well-designed entrances and exits can make, not just in how your space looks, but in how it feels and operates.

CHAPTER 12: TEMPORAL DYNAMICS: TIME IN ASTRAL ARCHITECTURE

Time: It's a construct that dominates our physical world, marking the seasons, dictating schedules, and shaping lives. But what about in the astral realm? As you step into the fabric of this ethereal space, do the hands of the clock tick the same way? This chapter delves into the peculiarities and manipulability of time in astral architecture. Understanding this can open up avenues for temporal designs that not only make your astral constructs more intricate but also more meaningful.

The Nature of Time in the Astral Plane

Time in the astral plane doesn't operate like it does in the physical world. The astral realm is a space of consciousness, a dimension where thoughts, emotions, and intentions carry a unique form of 'weight.' Because of this, time can be experienced more fluidly. Some travelers report feeling like they've spent hours in a place, only to discover mere minutes have passed in the physical world. Others speak of compressed experiences, where a wealth of wisdom is imparted in what seems like a blink of an eye.

This temporal flexibility offers architects a creative playground.

Imagine a temple where each room represents a different era or a garden that cycles through the four seasons within an astral day. Such creative freedom lets you develop constructs that provide deeply transformative experiences, unfettered by the linearity of earthly time.

Temporal Design Elements

- Chrono-thematic Rooms: Rooms that symbolically represent different epochs or time periods can create a journey through history or future possibilities. For instance, one could design an astral library where each section is dedicated to the wisdom of a particular century or civilization.

- Seasonal Gardens: Gardens that change their flora according to simulated astral 'seasons' can evoke unique energetic attributes beneficial for different types of meditation or spiritual work.

- Time Dilation and Contraction Spaces: Rooms designed to dilate or contract the subjective experience of time can be especially useful for deep meditation or spiritual exercises that require 'more time.'

Manipulating Astral Time

Some advanced practitioners claim to have developed methods for consciously manipulating time within their astral constructs. Techniques generally involve deep focus and the use of specific symbols or geometries known to represent time. For instance, using the Ouroboros (the ancient symbol of a serpent eating its tail) as a focal point in a room might serve to create a loop in time, allowing for a more extensive experience within a shorter 'objective' time frame.

Another way to manipulate time is through sound or vibrations, often achieved using astral 'instruments' that emit frequencies affecting the perception of time. These techniques are not universally verified but stem from traditions that give credence to the power of sound in metaphysical practices.

Ethical Considerations

Manipulating time in astral constructs may raise ethical questions, especially if shared with others. For instance, a temple designed to significantly dilate time might be overwhelming or disorienting for an inexperienced visitor. Always consider the potential psychological and spiritual impacts of your designs. In communal spaces, it's advisable to inform visitors of the temporal dynamics at play or to provide areas where time flows more conventionally for those who might need it.

Temporal Maintenance

An aspect often overlooked is the maintenance of temporal elements in astral architecture. Like any other feature, these elements can degrade or drift, requiring recalibration or 'tuning.' Regular visits and mental adjustments can help in maintaining the intended temporal dynamics.

In summary, the astral plane offers an array of possibilities when it comes to manipulating and experiencing time. Though the idea might seem foreign or even fantastical, incorporating temporal elements into your astral architecture enriches the depth and breadth of the experiences that these constructs can offer. While a full understanding of astral time dynamics is still beyond the scope of conventional science, anecdotal evidence and experiential reports from spiritual practitioners make a compelling case for its malleability and importance in astral design. So, as you plot the blueprints for your next astral sanctuary or temple, don't forget to ask yourself: What time is it in your astral world?

CHAPTER 13: SECURITY MEASURES: WARDING AND PROTECTING YOUR ASTRAL SANCTUARY

Welcome to Chapter 13, where we will delve into an often-overlooked but crucial aspect of astral architecture: security measures for warding and protecting your astral sanctuary. While the astral plane is generally a realm of spiritual growth and exploration, it's not devoid of challenges. Just as you'd take security precautions for your physical home, your ethereal constructions also need safeguarding against unwelcome energies or entities. In this chapter, we'll explore various methods for shielding your astral creations and maintaining a space conducive to spiritual and metaphysical endeavors.

Astral Security Concerns

While astral realms are often thought of as places for higher learning and self-discovery, they're not without their risks. Uninvited energies and entities can encroach upon your astral space, creating discord or even corrupting the integrity of what you've built. Additionally, as you venture deeper into astral realms, you may encounter beings whose intentions aren't aligned with your own spiritual objectives. These could range from minor nuisances to disruptive forces that can significantly affect your astral projects.

The Importance of Setting Intentions

The first line of defense in protecting your astral sanctuary begins with setting clear intentions. The energy of intention acts as a natural barrier that can repel inharmonious forces. When you're constructing your astral space, make sure you set explicit intentions for what the space is for and who is allowed to enter. This will serve as a basic warding technique and can deter any energies or entities that are not in sync with your stated purpose.

Energetic Boundaries and Shields

One effective way to protect your astral sanctuary is to establish energetic boundaries or shields. Just as you learned in Chapter 7 about crafting walls and boundaries in your astral architecture, you can imbue these physical constructs with specific protective energies. Picture a radiant force field emanating from the walls, floors, and ceilings of your astral structure. You can associate this energetic barrier with visual cues—such as glowing symbols or specific colors—to make it easier to maintain.

Utilizing Protective Symbols and Sigils

The use of protective symbols and sigils is a time-honored technique for warding off negative influences, both in the physical and astral realms. Symbols like the pentagram, the Eye of Horus, or customized sigils charged with your intentions can be integrated into your astral architecture for added security. By inscribing these symbols on walls or embedding them into the foundational structures, you create an additional layer of protection.

Guardian Entities and Spirit Allies

Some spiritual traditions recommend enlisting the aid of guardian entities or spirit allies to protect your astral space. These can range from ancestral spirits to mythological creatures like dragons or griffins. Invoking such guardians requires a strong foundation in ritual work and a respectful approach to these beings. Always remember that mutual respect and clear communication are essential when dealing with any entities in spiritual practices.

Advanced Warding Techniques

For those who have a strong foundation in metaphysical practices, advanced warding techniques like creating energy vortexes or setting up astral "alarms" can be employed. An energy vortex can act like a whirlpool, trapping and neutralizing negative energies. Astral alarms can alert you in your waking state or during other astral travels if your space is compromised.

Regular Maintenance

Like any other security measures, the wards and shields you put up will require regular maintenance. Energetic constructs can degrade over time or as they repel negative influences. Routinely reinforce your intentions, renew protective symbols, and check-in with any guardian entities you've enlisted. This upkeep ensures that your astral sanctuary remains a safe and harmonious space for your spiritual activities.

In summary, warding and protecting your astral constructions are vital aspects of astral architecture that serve to maintain the sanctity and purpose of your ethereal spaces. From setting clear intentions to utilizing advanced metaphysical techniques, multiple layers of security can be implemented to safeguard your astral endeavors. By taking the time to secure your astral sanctuary, you pave the way for more profound and uninterrupted spiritual growth and exploration.

CHAPTER 14: COMMUNAL CONSTRUCTS: BUILDING ASTRAL SPACES WITH OTHERS

Welcome to Chapter 14! While our journey so far has largely focused on individual endeavors within astral architecture, today we'll explore the fascinating terrain of collective astral building. If the idea of solo projects in the astral realm intrigued you, imagine what could be achieved when multiple minds come together, each contributing its unique creative spark. Community, after all, can enhance every experience, even those that exist in otherworldly planes.

The Power of Collective Consciousness

As we've touched upon earlier, the astral plane is very much influenced by thoughts, intentions, and consciousness. When more than one individual focuses on a specific astral construct, this amplifies the energy directed towards that structure. The result? A more potent and perhaps complex construction that has layers of meaning, enriched by the multitude of perspectives.

In various spiritual traditions and folklore, there are tales of collective spaces in the astral plane—shared temples, palaces of learning, or even entire landscapes fashioned by communal intent. These spaces often have heightened energy frequencies and are more intricately detailed due to the collective consciousness working in harmony.

Coordinated Astral Projection: How to Get There Together

When multiple people aim to reach the same astral space, it's essential to have coordinated methods for astral projection. Rituals, synchronized meditations, or shared visualizations can be very effective in ensuring everyone involved is "on the same page," so to speak.

Consider practicing together in the physical realm before taking the collective journey. Consistent methods and imagery ensure that all participants arrive in the same astral location. It can also be useful to designate roles for participants. One could serve as a "guide" or "architect," leading the way and laying out foundational constructs, while others could be "decorators," "builders," or even "guardians" focusing on protective energy.

Collective Blueprints: Designing Together

Designing a communal astral space requires a unique approach compared to individual projects. When multiple energies and intentions coalesce, it's vital to establish common goals and themes for the space you aim to build. Think of it as creating a master blueprint that accommodates the diverse but complementary contributions of each participant.

Before embarking on the actual construction, discuss the key features, layout, and intentions with your fellow builders. Will the space be a sanctuary for meditation, a temple for rituals, or a playground for astral adventures? Sketch out a preliminary design and allow room for individual improvisations.

Energetic Synergy: Balancing and Harmonizing

The harmony of energies is crucial in collective astral building. Each participant contributes unique energies to the space, and while diversity enriches the astral construct, it could also lead to discord if not properly balanced.

There are several techniques to harmonize energies. Rituals, chants, or shared visualizations can serve as bonding exercises, aligning energies before entering the astral plane. On reaching the designated astral location, consider placing collective "anchors"—constructs like shared symbols, crystals, or light sources that serve as the heart of the structure, stabilizing and harmonizing the environment.

Shared Maintenance and Upkeep

Once your communal astral space is up and running, maintenance becomes a shared responsibility. Regular "visits" by at least one of the participants can help sustain the structure's integrity. Scheduled group sessions can also be set up to cleanse, repair, or even expand the space. The continuity of collective attention ensures that the space thrives, becomes more potent, and serves its intended purpose effectively.

In Summary

Collective endeavors in astral architecture open up a world of possibilities that individual projects may not easily achieve. Through combined energies and shared visions, the astral constructs become more potent, rich, and versatile. The logistics might seem complex at first, but with practice and harmonious intent, they can lead to ethereal structures that are marvels of collective creativity. So, reach out to like-minded individuals and start brainstorming your next astral project. Who knows what celestial splendors you could construct when many hands—or minds, in this case—make ethereal work.

CHAPTER 15: CASE STUDIES: EXAMINING EXISTING ASTRAL ARCHITECTURES

Welcome to Chapter 15, a special segment where we move from theory and practice to real-life examples. We'll examine some well-known astral structures, highlighting their characteristics and discussing what makes them effective or sacred. These case studies will serve as practical illustrations of the principles we've discussed in previous chapters.

The Sanctuary of Elysian Light

In various accounts from practitioners experienced in astral projection, the Sanctuary of Elysian Light stands as a hallmark of intricate design and radiant energy. The space is often described as ethereal, bathed in light that seems to come from everywhere yet nowhere. Walls appear to be made of translucent crystals, and the geometry involved draws heavily from sacred forms—especially the Flower of Life and Metatron's Cube. It serves as a space of healing and enlightenment, often frequented by entities described as "beings of light."

The design incorporates elemental alchemy in a unique way, combining air and fire elements in the form of light and ether.

This Sanctuary is considered an advanced astral construct due to its manipulation of time; time dilation is often reported, making a few minutes in physical reality equivalent to what feels like hours in the astral realm. As for security measures, the Sanctuary is described as having a form of energetic screening, allowing only those with intentions of pure enlightenment and healing to enter.

The Labyrinth of Reflections

The Labyrinth of Reflections is another fascinating example, providing a stark contrast to the Sanctuary of Elysian Light. Here, the construct serves as a self-reflective journey for the traveler. It features intricately woven paths that lead to mirrors, not conventional mirrors but mirrors made of water or air. The walls are built using astral masonry techniques we've discussed, strong and made up of earthen elements.

Unlike the Sanctuary of Elysian Light, which is designed to elevate one's vibration, the Labyrinth seeks to confront the traveler with their own shadow, representing a more psychological and transformative approach. Elemental energies like water and earth are used to ground the practitioner. Time in this construct seems to flow in sync with one's emotional state, speeding up during moments of realization and slowing down during contemplation.

The Temple of the Ascended Masters

Often considered a collective project built by multiple advanced souls over what could be centuries in Earth time, the Temple of the Ascended Masters serves as a gathering point for high-level spiritual entities. It incorporates sacred geometry, particularly the phi ratio, and is said to exist in multiple dimensions simultaneously. The central hall has a spherical dome purportedly designed to harness cosmic energy.

Here, elemental alchemy is at its peak, with each section of the temple dedicated to one of the four elements. Moreover, transitional portals connect this temple to other astral locations, serving as a hub for multi-dimensional travel. Security here is said to be of the highest order, with energetic shields that are almost impenetrable, safeguarding the wisdom and higher vibrational frequencies within.

Shambhala: The Hidden Kingdom

Shambhala, while rooted in ancient Buddhist texts, has a presence in the astral realm according to numerous accounts. This mythical kingdom is an example of an astral construct built over centuries, perhaps even millennia, with the collective energy and intent of countless beings. Natural elements like gardens, waterfalls, and mountains coexist alongside temples and palaces.

It's a complex case because while it is described as an astral construct, many believe it also has a physical counterpart existing in a different dimensional frequency. Shambhala incorporates a harmonious balance between nature and architecture, a concept we discussed in Chapter 10.

Summary

These case studies offer insights into the variety of architectural styles, purposes, and complexities possible in astral constructs. From sanctuaries of healing to psychological labyrinths, from collective temples to mythical kingdoms, astral architecture offers a rich tapestry for spiritual exploration and enlightenment. Understanding existing astral constructs can help us refine our own projects, borrowing elements that resonate with our personal intentions and spiritual goals.

CHAPTER 16: ASTRAL MAINTENANCE: UPKEEP OF YOUR ETHEREAL CONSTRUCTIONS

In the journey we've been on, you've learned how to create beautiful, complex structures in the astral plane. Just like any physical building, your astral sanctuaries, temples, and landscapes also need regular care and maintenance. This chapter will explore the various ways to preserve the integrity, potency, and sacredness of your astral creations over time.

Ethereal Erosion: Understanding Decay

While it might seem that astral structures, existing in a non-physical realm, would be free from decay, this isn't entirely true. The astral realm is a plane of thought forms, emotions, and intentions. Consequently, your astral structures could be subject to what we might call "ethereal erosion." This erosion happens when the energies sustaining them—be it your focus, collective belief, or emotional investment—begin to wane.

The astral plane is also susceptible to the influences of

collective thought and cosmic cycles. Significant shifts in cosmic alignments, for instance, can affect the 'climate' of the astral realm, indirectly impacting the vitality of your constructs. Hence, a form of 'astral weathering' occurs, requiring timely maintenance to keep your structures robust.

Re-energizing Your Constructs

Regular visits to your astral constructions can keep them energized. Think of it as dusting your furniture or watering your plants in the physical world. Consistent interaction helps maintain the structure and may even enable it to evolve. In the astral realm, evolution often happens in a fluid and organic manner; you may find that a shrine becomes a temple, or a grove transforms into an entire forest. Your ongoing attention is like nourishment that enables such growth.

You can use rituals, meditation, and focused intent to recharge your constructs. Some practitioners use visual exercises like bathing their astral temple in light, imagining it strengthened by elemental forces, or simply engaging in activities within the space to reinforce its significance and vitality.

Repair and Redefinition

Erosion isn't the only factor that necessitates maintenance. Sometimes, the purpose of a space may change, calling for a redefinition or reconstruction. Just as we renovate our homes to serve new life stages, astral spaces too can be 'renovated.' Maybe the elemental balance needs readjustment, or perhaps new portals need to be opened as you access different realms.

Modifying an astral construct isn't just about "fixing" it. This process could be a transformative experience that broadens your spiritual understanding. As you edit, you might gain new insights into astral dynamics or uncover hidden aspects of yourself that were subconsciously woven into the original design.

Astral Cleaning and Protection

Sometimes, astral spaces can attract stray energies or thought-forms that you didn't intentionally invite. Regular cleansing rituals can keep your area free from such unintentional residents. Techniques such as astral smudging, using metaphorical 'salt' to purify, or creating protective barriers can be effective. This is akin to spiritual hygiene and can be as simple or as elaborate as you choose.

Scheduled Check-ins

Creating a schedule for astral maintenance can help. This doesn't mean you need a daily to-do list but having a rhythmic, ritualistic approach to visiting and upkeeping your astral constructs can help you build a robust relationship with them. Whether it's a weekly meditation or a monthly ritual, keeping to a schedule ensures your constructs remain not just intact but also vibrant.

Monitoring Elemental and Cosmic Shifts

As mentioned earlier, cosmic events and elemental shifts can affect your astral constructs. Keeping an eye on such occurrences can prepare you for necessary modifications. Some practitioners follow astrological cycles, lunar phases, or even larger cosmic cycles like solar flares, considering their potential influences on the astral realm.

To sum up, the astral structures you've built are more than mere figments of imagination; they're a part of your spiritual journey. They require the same care, attention, and respect that any sacred space in the physical world would demand. From understanding ethereal erosion to actively re-energizing and redefining your structures, astral maintenance is a multifaceted endeavor that assures the longevity and efficacy of your ethereal constructions. So, as you continue on your path as an architect of astral realms, remember that construction is just the beginning—the true essence lies in enduring guardianship and thoughtful upkeep.

CHAPTER 17: FROM ASTRAL TO PHYSICAL: MATERIALIZING ETHEREAL INSIGHTS

Welcome to Chapter 17, where we explore the bridge that connects the ethereal world of astral architecture to our material existence. The physical world can often seem cumbersome, constrained by laws of physics and socio-cultural norms. Yet, it is also where our corporeal selves reside, presenting endless opportunities for manifesting spiritual insights into physical forms. How then can we bring forth the wisdom and creative vibrance encountered in astral realms to enrich our earthly lives?

Spiritual Catalysts for Earthly Architecture

One of the most straightforward applications of astral architecture knowledge lies in the physical architecture of temples, churches, and other sacred spaces. Just as sacred geometry infuses astral designs with particular resonances, it can enhance the energy flow and spiritual ambiance of physical buildings. Even large-scale public projects like parks and city planning can incorporate such principles to promote harmony and well-being among its inhabitants.

Studying how energy circulates in your astral structures can inform how you might want to orient rooms or features in a physical space. The insight into elemental alchemy garnered from astral projects can offer a unique viewpoint on how to balance various elements, such as light and shadow, in real-world architectural design.

Creative Inspirations for Arts and Crafts

Your adventures in astral realms might not only influence large-scale projects but can also invigorate smaller-scale artistic endeavors. Whether you're a painter, musician, or writer, the ethereal landscapes and abstract concepts you encounter could be channeled into your art. The symbolic motifs used in your astral temples, for instance, can find their way into your storytelling or visual compositions, providing them layers of depth and meaning.

Grounding Astral Healing into Physical Practices

The astral plane can be an immense source of healing and rejuvenation. As you've learned, your astral sanctuary serves as a haven for spiritual growth, therapy, and emotional healing. However, the benefits need not stay on the astral plane. The techniques you've applied for directing energy, invoking elements, or channeling positive intentions in the astral can be adapted for use in physical healing modalities such as Reiki, acupuncture, or even conventional therapeutic settings. By incorporating these techniques, you can provide a multidimensional approach to healing that combines the best of both worlds.

Cognitive and Psychological Benefits

Engaging in astral architecture can also improve your problem-solving and imaginative skills, attributes that are highly valued in many professions. For example, the experience of building complex structures with intricate geometrical relationships can sharpen spatial awareness and abstract thinking. Additionally, the exercise of maintaining your astral creations enhances skills related to focus, discipline, and project management. These abilities are not only metaphysical treasures but also practical skills that can be applied in day-to-day living.

Ethical Considerations and Responsible Materialization

While it's exhilarating to bring astral insights into the physical realm, it's crucial to do so responsibly. Always consider the ethical implications of your actions. For instance, if you're using sacred geometry or specific cultural symbols in your designs, ensure you're doing so respectfully and with a proper understanding of their history and significance.

Also, bear in mind that while the astral plane may be boundless and less constrained by the laws of physics, our physical world has limitations. The materialization of any astral insights must respect the environment, contribute positively to communities, and align with the betterment of life on Earth.

Conclusion

The intricate, expansive universe of astral architecture isn't merely an esoteric field relegated to the confines of spiritual exploration. It is a fertile ground rich in insights that can profoundly impact various aspects of our earthly existence. From the grand designs of physical architecture and urban planning to the intimate realms of personal healing and artistic creation, astral experiences offer a myriad of opportunities for enriching our lives in tangible ways. By ethically and responsibly integrating these ethereal insights into our material world, we can begin to live more harmoniously, both within ourselves and with the world around us.

CHAPTER 18: CONCLUSION: THE FUTURE OF ASTRAL ARCHITECTURE

As we come to the close of this enlightening journey through the intricacies of astral architecture, it's important to take a moment to reflect on what the future might hold for this fascinating intersection of spirituality, metaphysics, and imaginative construction. Though we've covered an array of topics—from the basic principles of astral plane navigation to the complexities of sacred geometry and elemental alchemy—what lies ahead remains a domain rich with potential and challenges.

The Convergence of Technology and Spirituality

One of the most intriguing areas of future exploration is the role that technology may play in advancing our understanding and experience of the astral realm. Virtual reality, for instance, could become a tool for simulating astral spaces, serving as a training ground for those new to astral projection. While VR can't replicate the transcendental aspects of astral travel, it might offer a 'safe space' for people to practice visualization techniques and understand spatial constructs before attempting to project. It's a realm of "what-ifs" that bridges spirituality and technological innovation in a manner not previously considered.

Ethical Considerations in Astral Construction

As astral architecture becomes more widespread, ethical considerations will undoubtedly come into play. Questions about who has the right to construct in the astral realm, or whether collective spaces should be governed by some form of astral 'zoning laws,' may arise. Additionally, as with any form of construction—physical or astral—there is the concern for environmental impact. While the astral plane is not governed by physical laws as we understand them, it is an interconnected realm, and actions taken there could have repercussions we have yet to understand fully.

Astral Tourism and Cultural Preservation

As the idea of astral architecture gains more mainstream attention, it's plausible to foresee an uptick in 'astral tourism.' Much like visiting ancient temples or sacred sites in the physical world, individuals might embark on journeys to well-known astral constructs. This brings up concerns of cultural preservation. Would high-traffic astral constructs need "restoration" or protection from the wear and tear of frequent visits? Moreover, would there be a need to safeguard the integrity of ancient or culturally significant astral spaces from alteration or exploitation?

Accessibility and Inclusivity

As we move forward, making the practice accessible to a broader audience remains paramount. Astral architecture should not be the reserve of the few, but an open frontier for all those seeking spiritual enlightenment, solace, or even a bit of metaphysical adventure. Various schools of thought and cultural traditions may offer different methods or philosophies behind astral construction, contributing to a richer, more diverse astral landscape. By ensuring that resources and knowledge are shared openly, we can foster an environment of inclusivity.

Academic and Scientific Inquiry

While the nature of the astral realm defies conventional scientific analysis, the expansion of research into topics like consciousness, lucid dreaming, and even quantum theories of mind may provide frameworks for understanding the astral in ways we have not yet considered. The more we can validate aspects of astral projection and construction through interdisciplinary study, the closer we come to bridging the gap between skepticism and acceptance in academic circles.

In sum, the future of astral architecture is one rich with possibilities and ripe for exploration. The challenges are as monumental as the rewards, requiring a blend of spirituality, creativity, ethical consideration, and potentially even technological innovation. As we continue to push the boundaries of what is possible within the astral plane, we must proceed with both wonder and responsibility. After all, the astral realm is not just a space for individual exploration but a collective domain that we all have a stake in shaping. By approaching its development with care, respect, and a thirst for knowledge, we contribute to the spiritual and metaphysical tapestry that many generations will inherit and further enrich. So, as you close this book, remember: the realm of astral architecture does not end here; rather, it's just the beginning of what promises to be an extraordinary cosmic adventure.

THE END

Printed in Great Britain
by Amazon

37561558R00046